BEN E. EFE

Simple Ways To
SILENCE
THE VOICE OF THE
ENEMY

Simple Ways To Silence The Voice Of The Enemy

Life involves a consistent battle with the forces of darkness who speak and project evil into people's lives and destinies. But as a child of God, you have the grace to counter the voices and plans of the enemy against you.

It is true that the weapons of the enemies against you shall not prosper. But you have the responsibility of resisting and annulling every voice that rises against you in judgment.

This book will give you simple keys to empower your voice to quench and overcome all the plans and evil voices of the enemy against your life. Read it and live it! You are destined to win!

Ben E. Efe is the Senior Pastor of LivingWater Int'l Ministries (GRACE CENTRE), Ojodu-Lagos, a multi-faceted church committed to the transformation of lives and making people become what God wants them to be. He is also the president of Stay Alive, a ministry committed to the social and mental liberation of a regenerated society, empowering people to fulfill their destinies and potentials. He is a teacher, author, motivator and preacher whose message of hope and restoration have touched many lives in diverse ways. He graduated from the University of Ibadan, Nigeria with a degree in Philosophy and Political Science. He also attended the Redeemed Christian Bible College for postgraduate studies in Theology, and pastored New Heights Assembly of The Redeemed Christian Church of God, Ojodu, Lagos. Ben and his wife, Ese lives in Lagos, Nigeria.

Unless otherwise indicated, all scripture quotations are taken from the King James Version of the Holy Bible.

Scripture quotations marked NKJV are from the Holy Bible, New King James Version.

Scripture quotations marked WEB are from the World English Bible

Simple Ways to Silence The Voice Of The Enemy
- Ben E. Efe

Copyright © 2010 - Ben E. Efe

ISBN: 978 -0- 557- 45058 -9

A BEN E. EFE / STAY ALIVE BOOKS
efeben@yahoo.com,
stayalive_intl@yahoo.com
+234-8035125496, 8029309859
http://www.stayalivetips.blogspot.com
P. O. Box 22626, Ikeja, Lagos, Nigeria

All rights reserved. No part of this publication may be reproduced, stored in any retrieval system or by any means (electrical, mechanical, photocopying, recording or otherwise) without the prior authorization of the publisher except for brief printed reviews.

CONTENTS

Foreword v

PART ONE:
THE TWO VOICES OF LIFE

Chapter One
The Voice of The Enemy 9

Chapter Two
The Voice of Man (Your Voice) 18

PART TWO:
SIMPLE WAYS TO EMPOWER
YOUR VOICE

Chapter Three
Get Acquainted With God 27

Chapter Four
Be Filled With The Word of God 32

Chapter Five
**You Need A Change of
Heart & Repentance** 37

Chapter Six
You Need Hard Work 42

Chapter Seven
Worship The Lord 46

Chapter Eight
Pray Without Ceasing 52

Chapter Nine
Confess The Word. 58

Chapter Ten
Faith & A Right Attitude......................................62

Last Word!
True Power Over The Enemy..............................67

FOREWORD

"The heavens declare the glory of God; and the firmament sheweth his handywork. ² Day unto day uttereth speech, and night unto night sheweth knowledge. ³There is no speech nor language, where their voice is not heard. ⁴ Their line is gone out through all the earth, and their words to the end of the world. In them hath he set a tabernacle for the sun" (Psalm 19: 1- 4)

The Bible is a record of God speaking to man at different occasions. But just as God speaks, the devil speaks; man speaks; situations and circumstances of life speak; the elemental forces - sun, moon and stars speak. The water, fire and the earth speak.

The very fact that many of us cannot hear what these forces are transmitting does not mean there is no sound in the atmosphere. People who hear and understand what they project communicates with them.

This book in your hand becomes a very important tool of deliverance because whether or not you hear what the enemies have spoken to your life, the words are effective. On many instances, these words are negative and they have robbed many people of their destinies.

As you apply the simple principles in this book in your daily life, all the silent and audible voice of the enemy shall be silenced. Every evil pronouncement against your life shall be reversed.

In 1994, shortly after I bought a car, my neighbour and I were driving around town and we were listening to the 7:00am news on the car radio, when the exchange rate was announced by the newscaster. The figures were high and he told me to be careful with my car because many Nigerians may just be riding their last car. And I agreed with him. Afterwards, one thing led to another and I sold my car. And for many years I was without a car. I never forgot what he said that fateful day.

One day I recalled those words again and I realized that it was a 'strange voice' - the reason why I had been hindered. I rose up against it in prayers, confessing the word of God, and my situation changed.

Brethren, the enemy has a voice. But the voice of God will thunder against them as you read and practice the truth in this book. It is indeed a very simple and easy to read book with scriptural principles to silence the enemy's voice.

I strongly recommend it for all who desire to move forward in the journey of life.

-Pastor Samuel Abiodun Wright
Snr. Pastor,
Redeeming Hope Christian Centre
Baale-Ajuwon, Akute, Ogun State, Nigeria.

"No weapon that is formed against thee shall prosper; and every tongue that shall rise against thee in judgment thou shalt condemn. This is the heritage of the servants of the LORD, and their righteousness is of me, saith the LORD"

- Isaiah 54:17

PART 1:

THE TWO VOICES OF LIFE

Chapter One

The Voice of The Enemy

It is true that the number one enemy of a child of God is Satan the devil, the adversary.

Satan means "the hater, the opponent; the accuser, adversary or enemy, who hinders, obstructs and resists what is good".

Until he was driven away from heaven, he continually accused mankind before God. He spoke evil day and night, recounting peoples' failures and weaknesses in order to stop their blessings and well being.

The Bible says he is *"The accuser of our brethren is cast down, which accused them before our God day and night" (Rev 12:10).*

To accuse means to speak against; to testify against or to affirm a curse; and to throw up reasons, whether legal or not, to show that the accused person deserves punishment or some certain conditions.

This has been the ministry of Satan your enemy from time immemorial. He was part of the heavenly council and spoke directly to God accusing mankind.

Zechariah got this revelation when the Lord showed him how Satan opposed Joshua, the high priest.

"And he shewed me Joshua the high priest standing before the angel of the LORD, and Satan standing at his right hand to resist him"
(Zech 3:1)

"He showed me Joshua the high priest standing before the angel of Yahweh, and Satan standing at his right hand to be his adversary"
(Zech 3:1, WEB)

We also find the role of the accuser in the account of Job. God declared that Job was a perfect and upright man. But Satan poured out his venom to condemn him as an insincere worshipper of God with selfish motives for his uprightness. He indirectly meant Job was being good in order to gain God's blessings and protection, and without these blessings, Job would readily turn his back at God.

"And the LORD said unto Satan, Hast thou considered my servant Job, that there is none like him in the earth, a perfect and an upright man, one that feareth God, and escheweth evil? ⁹ Then Satan answered the LORD, and said, Doth Job fear God for nought? ¹⁰ Hast not thou made an hedge about him, and about his house, and about all that he hath on every side? thou hast blessed the work of his hands, and his substance is increased in the land"
(Job 1: 8-10).

To prove the devil wrong, God allowed him to test Job.

"But put forth thine hand now, and touch all that he hath, and he will curse thee to thy face. ¹² And the LORD said unto Satan, Behold, all that he hath is in thy power; only upon himself put not forth thine hand. So Satan went forth from the presence of the LORD"
(Job 1: 11-12).

*"And Satan answered the LORD, and said, Skin for skin, yea, all that a man hath will he give for his life. ⁵ But put forth thine hand

now, and touch his bone and his flesh, and he will curse thee to thy face. [6] And the LORD said unto Satan, Behold, he is in thine hand; but save his life" (Job 2: 4-6).

The passage above is the account of Satan's second attack on Job. And from that moment, the devil began to speak and wrought evil in the life of Job. And at every stage of the torment, his wicked voice reverberated to tell his havoc. *"While he was yet speaking"* was a recurring phrase to describe the serial attack on Job (Job 1:16, 17, 18).

We must realize that every attack of the enemy begins by a spoken word. Satan is a hater; therefore his is a direct opponent or opposite of God who is love! He wants to negate everything God does.

Remember too that if God wants to bless you, He does so by a spoken word. It is the spoken creative word of God that brings a blessing.

God revealed this to Moses when He instructed him to tell Aaron how to bless the people of Israel.

"And the LORD spake unto Moses, saying, ^{23} Speak unto Aaron and unto his sons, saying, On this wise ye shall bless the children of Israel, saying unto them, ^{24} The LORD bless thee, and keep thee: ^{25} The LORD make his face shine upon thee, and be gracious unto thee: ^{26} The LORD lift up his countenance upon thee, and give thee peace. ^{27} And they shall put my name upon the children of Israel; and I will bless them" (Num 6: 22-27).

The blessings of God come by the spoken word. In Genesis, He continually declared, *"Let there be"*, which culminated in the creation of man. The Bible says, *"He sent his word, and healed them, and delivered them from their destructions" (Ps 107: 20).*

On the contrary, the devil, enemy sends his words which David called arrows, and uses them to tempt people; to torment and weaken their faith, and to divert, delay and destroy their blessings.

This is also why **every problem or challenge of life has a voice.**

If you look at the challenges you are passing through or may have passed through, you would discover that they are not just silent. They speak fear, failure, barrenness, poverty, sickness, diseases, death, sorrow and so many other evils that disturb peoples' minds and lives.

In other words, if you are confronted by a challenge, that challenge would say something about you. For some people, the echo of the voice becomes very loud when the challenges has emptied their lives and overwhelm them.

For others who could muster some resistance, the sound is faint, but it is audible, because as long as the challenge remains, the voice will be heard, and as long as your window is open, the wind will blow.

For instance, if a person is sick, the enemy is speaking against his/ her physical well being; and until that voice is stopped, the person remains ill.

Many of the problems and challenges people go through are indeed strange voices which must be quenched.

The enemy, your enemy consistently and vehemently wants you to fail. That is why he continually speaks evil to tempt people, afflict their minds and discourage them.

The mind is one of the major targets of the devil's voice. He seeks to controvert people's believe and faith by projecting and speaking evil suggestions to cause them to have double minds and doubt God and His promises. And once the devil succeeds in doing this, the person becomes a victim he opposes and controls.

This is why a lot of people have bad habits and addictions which they even hate. Many do things they ordinarily would not do, and many people are baffled why particular sicknesses or evil occurrences continually recur in their lives.

One thing about your enemy is that, he is a tireless talker. He thrives on speaking evil and accusing people, and he continually goes about as a roaring lion seeking those he may devour (1 Pet 5:9).

But you can stop him. Yes, even though you cannot stop his ministry of moving to and fro looking for those to devour, you can stop him from coming near you and all that is yours. You can counter his voice with your voice.

DECLARATIONS / PRAYERS

1. I resist and bind every satanic voice attempting to sabotage my destiny, in Jesus' name.

2. Holy Ghost fire, arise and consume every plan of the enemy to stop good things in my life, in Jesus' name.

3. I take authority over every tongue attempting to speak against my blessings, goodness and peace even before their manifestation. I command you to fall and die, in Jesus' name.

4. I overcome the enemies confiscating and diverting the blessings of my life, in Jesus' name.

5. I barricade my life and destiny from the voice, arrows and manipulations of the enemy, in Jesus' name.

6. Every voice of discouragement, oppression and deception planning to shift me from my God's ordained place of blessing and peace, I say be frustrated and die in Jesus' name!

7. I decree in the mighty name of Jesus, that no seed sown by the voice of the enemy shall bear fruit in my life. I curse your root to die permanently in Jesus' name.

8. I am the anointed of God, no evil voice and plan can stop my dream, my finances, my health, my marriage and destiny.

Chapter Two

The Voice of Man (Your Voice)

The voice of man (a child of God) is a direct reverberation of the voice of God which speaks good and blessings.

The voice of God connotes His authority and power, and once He speaks, it accomplishes whatsoever He wills. David said, *"God hath spoken once; twice have I heard this; that power belongeth unto God" (Ps 62:11).*

Jesus Christ also affirmed this when He said, *"For thine is the kingdom, and the power, and the glory, for ever" (Matt 6: 13).*

Since no one can contest the truth that all power belongs to God, it behoves us to wield that authority and power because we are His direct representatives and ambassadors. We carry His Spirit and are created in His image. And He has infused that ability to use our voice the same way He would.

Jesus Christ said He has given us a voice that will subdue our enemies.

"For I will give you a mouth and wisdom, which all your adversaries shall not be able to gainsay nor resist" (Luke 21:15)

He has also given us the grace to overcome all powers of darkness.

"Behold, I give unto you power to tread on serpents and scorpions, and over all the power of the enemy: and nothing shall by any means hurt you"
(Luke 10: 19)

Note that the ability to tread upon your enemies (serpents and scorpions) is embedded in your voice through the name of Jesus. The 70 disciples told the Master, *"Lord, even the devils are subject unto us through thy name" (Luke 10: 17)*.

As a child of God, the redemption by the blood of Jesus Christ gives you a special authority and position which enables you to confront and defeat the devil and his agents. But you need to enforce that authority by your word, publicly declaring or confessing your faith.

"And they overcame him by the blood of the Lamb, and by the word of their testimony; and they loved not their lives unto the death" (Rev. 12:11)

"The word of their testimony" means the authority of God's word; and this is your number one key to victory.

Apostle Paul also tell us in Ephesians that after the battle (or wrestle) of life and death against principalities and powers (Eph 6:12), we need to use the armour of God; and the chief offensive weapon in this armour is the sword of the Spirit, which is *rhema*, the spoken Word of God.

If you must win the battle of life and enjoy your ordained blessings, you must engage your mouth and switch on the power and authority in God's word.

No matter the evil the enemy has spoken into your life, which may be raging at this moment, you can rebuke and silence it by your voice.

To rebuke means "to speak severely to somebody because they have done something wrong".

Beloved, you cannot continue to tolerate or endure the arrows of the enemy. You must rebuke him. The devil is a recalcitrant recidivist who would not lie low or surrender quietly, so you must continually rebuke him sternly. That is the only language he understands. Don't reason or argue with him; just resist and rebuke him!

When the devil troubled Joshua, the high priest, God rebuked him.

> **"And the LORD said unto Satan, The LORD rebuke thee, O Satan; even the LORD that hath chosen Jerusalem rebuke thee: is not this a brand plucked out of the fire?" (Zech 3:2)**

I don't know for how long the enemies may have troubled you; let them begin to hear your voice. Speak to them.

For you to overcome the evil plans of the enemy over your life, **you need to counter the voices with your superior blessed voice.** You need to condemn them.

When Goliath confronted David, his first attack on David was by a spoken word intended to put David under a curse and make evil befall him.

> *"And the Philistine said unto David, Am I a dog, that thou comest to me with staves? And the Philistine cursed David by his gods. ^{44} And the Philistine said to David, Come to me, and I will give thy flesh unto the fowls of the air, and to the beasts of the field" (1 Sam 17: 43-44)*

Shadrach, Meshach, and Abednego were threatened by Nebuchadnezzar, *"…if ye worship not, ye shall be cast the same hour into the midst of a burning fiery furnace; and who is that God that shall deliver you out of my hands?" (Dan 3:15).*

But the young men were wise enough to annul the voice of the evil king. They said, *"If it be so, our God whom we serve is able to deliver us from the burning fiery furnace, and he will deliver us out of thine hand, O king. 18 But if not, be it known unto thee, O king, that we will not serve thy gods, nor worship the golden image which thou hast set up" (Dan 3: 17-18).*

As a child of god, you are duty bound to counter and condemn the voice (plans) of the enemy against your life. Though the voice of God (His Word) ultimately puts a seal of protection upon your life and destiny, you still have to play your own part by wielding your authority.

The Bible emphatically says, **"No weapon that is formed against thee shall prosper; and every tongue that shall rise against thee in judgment thou shalt condemn. This is the heritage of the servants of the LORD, and their righteousness is of me, saith the LORD" (Isa 54: 17)**.

There are two inherent and instructive truths in this scripture. It implies that God's protective voice or power is over you. If anyone wishes, let him or her go to the moon or into the ocean to concoct any charm, or speak any evil against you; it <u>shall</u> fail. It would be an adventure in futility.

But this scripture implies another truth. God wants us to use our voice, which is our confrontational power or authority. It says, **"Every tongue that shall rise against thee in judgment thou shalt condemn"**!

For God to foil evil plots and accusations against you, you have to rise to condemn them. God says it is your heritage, your right; therefore you must use it.

The reason why many people allow the enemy to continually cheat them and perpetuate his evils in their lives is because of ignorance, and secondly because of the lack of faith, which makes our voices weak even when we use them to resist and counter the enemy.

For your voice to ultimately put the enemy where he belongs, it must be empowered, renewed, anointed and used wisely.

If your words are not of power, they would be meaningless to the devil. He would readily ignore them and continue to inflict injuries on you.

DECLARATIONS / PRAYERS

1. I've been set free by the Blood of Jesus and I refuse to be bound!

2. Every hold of the enemy manipulating my life, I break you now, in Jesus' name.

3. Every instrument of intimidation and oppression, I say be disgraced out of my life, in Jesus' name.

4. Every pronouncement, spell or plan meant to bring misfortune and failure to my life, I command you to turn to blessings, in Jesus' name.

5. In the mighty name of Jesus, I cancel every decree of untimely death issued against my life.

6. I release the ministering angels to pursue and scatter every gang up of evil voices against my destiny, in Jesus' name.

7. Every spirit of toiling released to hinder my life, I come against you by fire, in Jesus' name.

8. Every spoken evil and wicked spirit hiding in my life, waiting to hinder me at the point of breakthrough, I command you to come out and be destroyed, in Jesus' name.

PART 2:

SIMPLE WAYS TO EMPOWER YOUR VOICE

Chapter Three

Get Acquainted With God

"Acquaint now thyself with him, and be at peace: thereby good shall come unto thee"
(Job 22: 21)

There are so many voices in the world, but only the counsel of the Lord stands supreme. And once you team up with Him, He empowers you to do exploit as He does.

To acquaint yourself with Him literally means to become born-again and stay born-again. To be acquainted means, "to be familiar with something or somebody, having seen or experienced him". In other words, it means to have an encounter with God through Jesus Christ's redemption.

If you become acquainted with God by fellowship or become born-again, He bestows power and authority on you, which can withstand any arsenal of the enemy.

"But as many as received him, to them gave he power to become the sons of God, even to them that believe on his name" (John 1:12)

Many people whine and cry due to the torment and harassment of the devil and his agents. But if you are not born-again, the devil has legitimate power to oppress you, because if you are not on God's side, you are invariably on your own, left to the control and manipulation of the devil.

Jesus Christ said, *"He who is not with Me is against Me, and he who does not gather with Me scatters abroad" (Matt 12:30).* What this means is, if you are not on the side of the Lord, you are indirectly opposed to His mission, and no peace or good can come to you.

If you want to receive goodness in spite of the evil declarations of the enemy concerning your life, then you must make peace with God through Jesus Christ.

The Bible says, *"we have peace with God through our Lord Jesus Christ" (Rom 5:1).*

This peace removes the barriers between us (in our sinful nature) and God. It brings an end to hostility and unites us with God (Eph. 2:14). And once you get united with God, it becomes an abomination for the enemy to go against you.

"What shall we then say to these things? If God be for us, who can be against us?" (Rom 8: 31) This is one profound assurance of God's security and protection.

If you are acquainted with the Lord, He comes and live inside of you, and in this new state, no enemy can trample upon you. You only need to accept Jesus and continually believe in Him and affirm your faith.

Your status as a born again child of God plus your faith puts you beyond the reach of the voice and plans of the enemy.

"For whatsoever is born of God overcometh the world: and this is the victory that overcometh the world, even our faith. [5] Who is he that overcometh the world, but he that believeth that Jesus is the Son of God?" (1 John 5:4-5).

If you are acquainted with the Lord, or have had personal encounter with Him and you are born again, believe that no enemy or challenge can conclusively defeat you or overcome you. You have been empowered by God. Address the enemy and the challenges in your life with that confidence.

The grace, right, power and authority have been bestowed on you as a child of God.

"Ye are of God, little children, and have overcome them: because greater is he that is in you, than he that is in the world" (1 John 4:4)

DECLARATIONS /PRAYERS

1.   I release the fire of God against every negative impression or image painted of my life by the forces of darkness to project backwardness and sorrow.

2.   I overcome every habit or spirit interfering with my service, worship and obedience of God.

3.   I resist and cast away every satanic attempt to sabotage my destiny and rob me of the joy of salvation.

4.   Everything or path the enemy has made crooked in my life, I command you to be straightened, in Jesus name.

5.   I decree failure and shame over the plans of the enemy to lure me away from the will of God, in Jesus name.

6.   I am born of God; therefore no plan or chain of the enemy can tie me down. I'm destined for victory, in Jesus name!

7.   I refuse to be what the enemy wants me to be!

8.   Oh Lord, contend with the enemies of my life - Isa 49: 25-26

Chapter Four

Be Filled With The Word

"Receive, I pray thee, the law from his mouth, and lay up his words in thine heart"
(Job 22: 22)

One major significant reason why the devil still threatens and overwhelms many people is basically the lack of knowledge.

If you do not know your right or appreciate who you are as a child of God, the enemy will have a free reign in tormenting your mind.

It is sad that so many Christians and non Christians alike have at least a copy of the Bible; but very few people truly live by the truth and grace which the Word offers. This is why when challenges and tough times comes, people are easily swayed, afraid, discouraged and tend to go back on their faith.

The Bible says we should *"...hold fast the profession (confession) of our faith without wavering; (for he is faithful that promised)" (Heb 10: 23).* But how can we profess our faith if we do not know or understand what we are entitled to.

The devil is a liar; but he cannot controvert the truth of God's word. And the word is your number one weapon against the enemy.

When he fires his evil arrows at you, you have the word of God to counter them. The word puts every attack of the enemy in check. Without the word, you are defenseless and powerless, like a soldier at the warfront without a weapon.

The responsibility of knowing the word rests with you. The Bible says, *"Lay up His words in your heart" (Job 21:22, NKJV).*

To lay means to pile up or to store up deliberately for future use. This is what the psalmist meant when he said, *"Thy word have I hid in mine heart, that I might not sin against thee" (Ps 119:11).*

You need to diligently practice God's word by meditating on it as God instructed Joshua.

"This Book of the Law shall not depart from your mouth, but you shall meditate in it day and night, that you may observe to do according to all that is written in it. For then you will make your way prosperous, and then you will have good success"
(Jos 1:8, NKJV)

If you pile up God's word in your heart and follow or obey its instructions, it would continually put you ahead of the devil and his gimmicks.

If you are a doer of God's word and the word abides in you, you can and will compel the enemy to bring back all he has stolen from you. You can place a barrier between him and your blessings; and you can ultimately overcome every of his evil plans.

In spite of the diabolic voices and plans of the enemy against your life, the word of God will make you excel and "be like a tree planted by the channels of water".

Take time to study the word - dig deep. Your blessings are enshrined and embedded in it. It has the solution to all of life's problems. It will embolden you. It will build and strengthen your faith, and open your eyes to see and appreciate what God has in stock for you. And with its revelation, you can douse and quench every pronouncement and harassment of the enemy.

I have had personal experiences where passages I spoke from the Bible to the dead brought back life; brought healing, deliverance; restored broken relationships; turned fortunes around, and wrought miracles. Truly the word works wonders!

For instance, the truth and revelation of Psalm 18 is enough for you to shame your enemy. It was a song and testimony of David when the Lord delivered him from the hand of all his enemies including Saul.

DECLARATIONS / PRAYERS

1. Oh Lord, let your word become fire in my mouth, and let it consume the enemies of my life and destiny, in Jesus' name.

2. I am free from any generational or legal curse; and I free myself from every evil family trend, in Jesus' name.

3. According to your word (Ps 18: 14) send out your arrows and lightening to scatter and blind all the enemies of my life, in Jesus' name.

4. I -------------------------------(add your name) is a child of the living God. I command every stranger speaking against my life to surrender now, in Jesus' name Ps 18: 44.

5. Every secret problem hiding in my life, I command you to be exposed and destroyed permanently by fire, in Jesus' name.

6. In the mighty name of Jesus, every enemy standing against me, be broken to pieces Jer 30: 16.

7. I annul every decision, decree or counsel perfected by the enemy against my destiny. They shall neither stand nor come to pass, in Jesus' name Isa 8: 10.

8. I break, reject and cast down every stronghold of the enemy perpetuating failure, sickness, barrenness, discouragement and sorrow in my life.

Chapter Five

You Need A Change of Heart & Repentance

"If you return to the Almighty, you will be built up" **(Job 22: 23, NKJV)**

The devil knows the weaknesses of so many people, and as an accuser of brethren, he uses these weaknesses against them.

When people fall into one sin or the other by falling for the temptation of the devil, he turns around to use their error to torment and mock them. "Do you think God will ever hear your prayers again?" "So you call yourself a child of God?"

This is why some people run away from God, from His presence and from church when they fall. This is wrong. The enemy wants to drive you farther away from God, from His protection in order to expose you to his own arrows and attack.

If you ever fall into sin, don't run away from God. Rather, run to Him and go on your knees! When you run away, you indirectly shed your garment of sonship like the Prodigal Son in Luke 15.

In an estranged state, you can never wield your authority over the enemy because you surrender it by running away from God.

Sin weakens and douses the authority and grace of God upon our lives. It reduces us to the level of the enemy; and once you drop to his terrain, you can never defeat him in his domain.

It is not uncommon for a Christian to fall into sin. But don't let the enemy drive you deeper into sin. Repent quickly.

God does not close the door to a fallen child. But if you allow the devil to pull you further away, he would turn you to a victim and a toy manipulated by his wicked voice.

"If my people, which are called by my name, shall humble themselves, and pray, and seek my

face, and turn from their wicked ways; then will I hear from heaven, and will forgive their sin, and will heal their land" (2 Chro 7:14)

Sin is like when a man carries a basket full of pebbles and throws them into the sky above him. He is likely to be hit by the dropping stones. Whenever you sin or do any evil, you will eventually feel the negative effect.

This is why the Bible says, *"He who digs a pit will fall into it, And whoever breaks through a wall will be bitten by a serpent. 9 He who quarries stones may be hurt by them, And he who splits wood may be endangered by it"* (Eccl 10: 8-9) See Proverbs 26: 27.

Sin degrades a man and reduces him to a slave. It breaks down his defenses and shatters God's protective seal and shield. But if you return to God or repZent, He builds you up and restores you to your original position where the enemy cannot dominate your life.

Repentance brings a threefold grace. God <u>hears</u> you in spite of the enemy's accusations. He <u>forgives</u> you. And He <u>heals</u> or repairs and restores you.

Don't let the devil rubbish your life because of sin. Don't let him dominate your affairs. Don't let him mock or scoff at your testimonies and blessings. You are a child of God. Return to Him; change your ways; trust him and obey His word.

If you truly must walk over your enemies and the challenges of life, you must first walk with God. But *"Can two walk together, except they be agreed?" (Amos 3:3)*

Return to God. Remember that until the Prodigal Son changed his mind and returned to his father (where he truly belonged) he remained a slave and a beggar, whose best was companionship with pigs.

DECLARATIONS / PRAYERS

1. I repent of every presumptuous sin of pride, of relying on my own strength, of faithlessness, and I ask for the grace to please you, oh Lord.

2. I resist every ungodly agenda drawing me away from the purpose of God.

3. I refuse to bow to the wishes of my enemies, in Jesus' name.

4. I renounce every covenant with ungodly spirits Jezebel, ancestral spirits, etc.

5. I reject and renounce every satanic name the enemy has used to intimidate and manipulate my life.

6. I receive God's divine intervention in every area of my where I have failed.

7. Every satanic load or hindrances limiting my life and bending my destiny out of shape, your end has come. I say be destroyed in Jesus' name!

8. I lose myself completely from every manipulating voice and satanic oppression, in the mighty name of Jesus!

Chapter Six

You Need Hard Work

"Then shalt thou lay up gold as dust..."
(Job 22: 24)

In life, there are many people with great dreams; but the world celebrates only achievers. Truly, every man is bestowed with at least one potential and gift. But if you fail to use them or deliberately and lazily procrastinate and wait for conditions to be easy, favourable and perfect before you act to change your life, then you would remain a victim of the devil and challenges of life.

The reason why a lot of people are frightened by the voices of hardship, tough times and failure is because they are lazy and refuse to work hard.

If you have laboured and worked hard, the devil cannot scare you, because God will indeed bless the work of your hands.

In parable of the wheat and tares (in Matt 13: 24-30), the Bible says. *"...But while men slept, his enemy came and sowed tares among the wheat, and went his way"*. The enemy chose the night time because it is a time when men are seemingly defenseless, unvigilant and carefree.

But the Sower was unperturbed by the discovery of the evil act against him. He told the harvesters to ignore the tares, because he had done his homework well ahead. The Bible says he *"sowed good seed in his field" (Matt 13:24)*. He was therefore confident that in spite of the plans of the enemy, his good seed (good works) will stand the test of time.

Truly, nothing pays like hard work, commitment to duty and deliberate diligence in your affairs. Refuse to be lazy!

"Seest thou a man diligent in his business? he shall stand before kings; he shall not stand before mean men" (Pro 22:29)

If you are hard-working and you are a person committed to setting goals and planning your life and commit your affairs to God, the enemy cannot scare or discourage you. Whether there is economic recession, inflation, famine, plagues and other unexpected and untoward happenings, you would not be moved.

But you must be ready to work hard. Remember that, even if you are in the so-called God's own country (USA), you would not pick gold on the streets; neither do they do so in Gold Coast. You must work hard and smartly too. Remember also that, God gives us apples and not apple juice. He would give you shoes; but you have to tie the shoe laces yourself.

DECLARATIONS / PRAYERS

1.　I command every hidden potential in me to come alive now, in Jesus' name.

2.　I shall find pleasure in hard work and I shall not be lazy.

3.　Oh Lord, bless the work of my hands that I may not labour in vain.

4. I command every stone rolled on my path of breakthrough to fall and hit the senders, in Jesus' name.

5. I command every satanic padlock blocking the door to my success to break, in Jesus' name.

6. I overcome and pull down every gate, obstacle or barrier between me and my ordained blessings.

7. I receive the power / grace to rise from failure to glory; from barrenness to fruitfulness; from sorrow to joy, in Jesus' name.

8. The Lord that began a good work in me shall perfect it in Jesus' name.

Chapter Seven

Worship

"For then shalt thou have thy delight in the Almighty, and shalt lift up thy face unto God"
(Job 22: 26)

The several and incessant attacks of the enemy is intended to make you disbelief God and drive you to sin against Him.

The majority of sin or disobedience to God's word is rooted in lack of faith - a disbelief of His purpose, will and plan for our lives. And this is what the devil vehemently seeks to achieve through his afflictions, temptations and instigated and perpetuated challenges.

The only true way you can defeat the enemy in this regard and silence him is to worship God.

To worship simply means to express reverence for God; to show respect or strong feeling of love.

To worship also means to bow, to lie or fall down when paying homage to God. This means to utterly surrender to God. This was what Abraham did when he completely offered and surrendered his only son for a burnt offering to God. He said,

"...I and the lad will go yonder and worship..."
(Gen 22:5)

We must realise that whenever we allow God to have His way in our lives, the result will lead to our very own good. Following God's will eventually lead to your will being fulfilled. But the devil will not allow this. He wants us to do things independent of God so that we become exposed to his attacks and manipulations.

Abraham desired a blessing from God, and when he chose to worship Him with all he had (Isaac), God blessed him with the ultimate blessing that finally silenced the enemy concerning his destiny.

There are five things worthy of note about Abraham.

1.   He was eager to worship God. He surrendered all to Him (Gen 22:1)

2. He gave God's worship first place in his heart (Gen 22:2)
3. He was willing to give his best possession his only son!
4. His obedience was instant, in that, "he rose up early…" to do as he was commanded by God
5. He had extraordinary faith in God whom he surrendered all to, therefore he declared, *"I and the lad will go yonder and worship…"* (Gen 22:5)

Abraham worshipped God in faith and rather than restoring only Isaac to him, God gave him uncountable seed.

"…in blessing I will bless thee, and in multiplying I will multiply thy seed as the stars of the heaven, and as the sand which is upon the sea shore; and thy seed shall possess the gate of his enemies" (Gen 22: 17).

When you worship God, He is committed to loving and blessing you. His word says, *"I love them that love me; and those that seek me early shall find me"* (Pro 8:17).

Another way of worshipping God which many people treat with levity is tithing.

When you pay your tithes, you surrender your finances to God. But this is seemingly too difficult for many Christians, and the devil have held many captive due to their ignorance or erroneous beliefs about tithing. And for some, their utter disobedience and disregard for God's word prevents them from enjoying the best of God.

A major blessing attached to worshipping God with your finances is found in Malachi 3: 10 &11.

> *"Bring all the tithes into the storehouse, That there may be food in My house, And try Me now in this," Says the LORD of hosts, "If I will not open for you the windows of heaven And pour out for you such blessing That there will not be room enough to receive it.* [11] *"And I will rebuke the devourer for your sakes, So that he will not destroy the fruit of your ground, Nor shall the vine fail to bear fruit for you in the field," Says the LORD of hosts"*
> *(Mal 3: 10-11, NKJV)*

To *"rebuke the devourer for your sakes"* means that every blessing and goodness which you are entitled to shall be directed to you and no enemy, not even Satan can hinder or stop it.

Perhaps why the enemy is still toying with our finances is because we have neglected the plan of God for us through tithing.

Tithes and offering is a strong means of worship which quenches the voice of your enemies concerning your finances, health and general well being.

DECLARATIONS / PRAYERS

1. That evil vehicle transporting sorrow, failure, shame and satanic counsel into my life, I command you to catch fire, in Jesus' name.

2. Every plan of the enemy to quench my joy and testimony shall fall flat, in Jesus' name.

3. The evils fashioned against me shall bow before the blessings of God in my life.

4.   No satanic lie will tempt me from worshipping the Lord.

5.   No blessing ordained for me shall pass me by, in Jesus' name.

6.   The Lord will fill my mouth with new songs, in Jesus' name.

7.   No matter what the enemy say or does, everything shall turn around for my good to the glory of God!

8.   The Lord will continually show Himself big and strong on my behalf, in Jesus' name.

Chapter Eight

Prayer Without Ceasing

"Thou shalt make thy prayer unto him, and he shall hear thee" (Job 22: 27)

Usually, what the enemy does by speaking evil into people's lives is to hinder their destiny, distort or divert their blessings and goodness.

He recounts people's weaknesses, mistakes and sins, and amplifies them before God with intent to stop God's flow of grace and blessing to people's lives.

But as a child of God, you have the grace and privilege to call upon God to counter the evil arrows and assault of your enemy.

Prayer creates a path and opening where there is none, or where the enemy has closed doors to you. It turns stumbling blocks into stepping stones.

What the enemy does by his accusations, temptations and afflictions is to box you into a corner where you would feel lonely, forsaken and exposed to his attacks. But God does not want you to go about wearing sullen look of guilt, defeat and condemnation. Jesus died for us to create an avenue for us to experience profound intimate and personal relationship with God through prayers.

The question however is, "do you really believe God answers your prayers?" In ministry, I have come across several people who have lost hope and given up on life and surrendered to the enemy simply because they don't know how to call upon God to intervene in their situations. Yet the word of God is clear on this issue, if only we believe what it says.

> *"The LORD hear thee in the day of trouble; the name of the God of Jacob defend thee; ^{2} Send thee help from the sanctuary, and strengthen thee out of Zion" (Psalm 20: 1-2)*

> *"Give us help from trouble: for vain is the help of man. ^{12} Through God we shall do valiantly: for he it is that shall tread down our enemies" (Psalm 60: 11-12)*

> ***"Thou art my King, O God: command deliverances for Jacob. ⁵ Through thee will we push down our enemies: through thy name will we tread them under that rise up against us" (Psalm 44: 4-5)***

The challenge of so many people is that their minds are cluttered up and they allow situations to overwhelm them to the extent that they don't appreciate that God is just a prayer away.

A simple, "help me Lord" prayer in faith can turn your situation around. But sadly, many people allow the enemy to complicate things for them. Prayer is never meant to be very complicated or complex.

You don't need to wait to get to a special place, at a special time before you call upon God. Too many people use religion to hinder themselves.

Religiosity interferes with your relationship with God because it is confusing and makes your Father less accessible. This gladdens the enemy because it slows down your breakthrough.

The instruction to "pray without ceasing" is not a complex religious principle. It simply means to trust God for everything (big or small) and ask Him to change our lives **at all times.** Though trials and tests may yet persist, praying always will give you unique joy and peace. This way, the scripture Phil 4:6 will become real to you.

> ***"Be anxious for nothing, but in everything by prayer and supplication, with thanksgiving, let your requests be made known to God" (Phil 4:6, NKJV)***

If you want to continually silence the enemy of your life, all you need is a simple prayer of faith. Talk to the Lord always about everything. Stop carrying all that burden by yourself. Hand them over to God. This is what God expects of you. Remember Jesus said,

> ***"Take my yoke upon you, and learn of me; for I am meek and lowly in heart: and ye shall find rest unto your souls. ^{30} For my yoke is easy, and my burden is light" (Matt 11: 29 -30)***

DECLARATIONS / PRAYERS

1. I thank you Lord for this is my season of divine remembrance.

2. I thank you Lord, for all my spiritual blessings shall begin to have earthly manifestation, in Jesus' name.

3. I thank you Lord for you will continually frustrate the plans of the enemy to bring hardship, sorrow and pain to my life.

4. Every goodness the enemy has stolen from me, I claim you back, in Jesus' name.

5. Heavenly Father, continually expose and disgrace the voice of the enemy over my life.

6. Every power, force or personality opposed to good things in my life, I command you to be silent, in Jesus' name.

7. Oh Lord, every left over of satanic manipulations, curses and covenants that had hindered my life, I bring them before your throne of judgment now, in Jesus' name!

8. Heavenly Father, I receive the grace to become what you want me to be, in Jesus' name.

Chapter Nine

Word Confession

"Thou shalt also decree a thing, and it shall be established unto thee: and the light shall shine upon thy ways" (Job 22: 28)

It is one thing to speak to a situation; it is another to speak the right words. Condemning the enemy and his judgment and weapons fashioned against you is more than just speaking or barking commands or decrees.

Issuing decrees against the enemy is only effective if you speak the word of God and speak them rightly. It is like hitting a nail into a thick wood. If you don't hit it precisely, you won't drive the nail in.

The word of God is indeed like a hammer and as you hit at the head of your enemies, sooner than later, they would be destroyed.

> *"Is not my word like as a fire? saith the LORD; and like a hammer that breaketh the rock in pieces?" (Jer 23: 29)*

If you don't hold the hammer properly, your efforts in using the word would be futile and even injurious. Do you have a moral ground to wield or use God's word? Do you belong to God?

> *"He that hath my word, let him speak my word faithfully" (Jer 23: 28)*

You cannot bind the devil with your mouth and yet hold on to his properties. You cannot command the devil to get out of your marriage when you sleep with other people's spouse. You cannot decree a thing with your mouth and yet accommodate the devil and darkness in your heart.

The word of God is not theory or just any talk or ordinary word. It is spirit and life. It is light.

Speaking the word would only become effective if we live the life God wants us to live, whether we like it or not.

When the devil wants to steal, kill, destroy or afflict a soul, he begins by speaking darkness. In order to counter him and his forces, you must resort to speaking the Light of God - the Word.

When the devil attempted to derail Jesus Christ in the wilderness, the Lord simply responded, *"It is written" (Matt 4: 4)*. That word was more alive, more powerful and sharper than the tricks and darkness of the enemy.

Too often we struggle in and with darkness when all we should do is switch on God's light - His Word (logos) and confess or speak it (rhema) over our lives.

A lot of people live dissatisfied and frustrated lives simply because they carry about the logos without using it. God did not create us with unique gifts and grace to just go through life living at the mercy of challenges and the enemy. As Christians, we have the power of God inside of us, and we should have the brightest of lives.

Make up your mind to take hold of God's word; chew it, eat it, and speak it! And light will shine upon the affairs of your life.

DECLARATIONS / PRAYERS

1. No principality or territorial demon will have dominion over me and my destiny, in Jesus' name.

2. My finances shall be what God wants it to be!

3. Every attempt by any one to ruin my life and destiny shall back fire, in Jesus' name.

4. Those that gather against me shall eat their own flesh and suck their own blood, in Jesus' name.

5. This year, the glory of God shall manifest in my life, marriage and destiny, in Jesus' name.

6. I shall not dance to any music of sorrow, darkness, sickness, failure or death played by the enemy!

7. The blessings and the Word of God shall not be prolonged (or delayed in my life) when its manifestation comes.

8. All flesh shall see the glory of God in my life, in Jesus' name.

Chapter Ten

Faith And A Right Attitude

"When men are cast down, then thou shalt say, There is lifting up; and he shall save the humble person." (Job 22: 29)

So you have been afflicted. You are jobless and perhaps penniless. So you are childless and perhaps frustrated in one way or the other. But who are you?

You are the child of God! The sooner you realize this and stop teasing yourself, the better and easier it is for you to silence the voice and deception of the enemy.

One of the greatest weapons the enemy uses against people is fear. If he can get you to fear and lose faith, you would doubt God and eventually disobey Him.

The enemy knows that faith is what makes you pleasing to God; therefore he would continually strive to douse your faith and break your resolve to trust God. He would make you feel inadequate and unworthy of God's love. He would discourage and tempt you at every opportunity.

But you must hold your grounds by faith and a right attitude. This way, your voice will silence every suggestion, accusation and enterprise of the enemy against you.

No matter your condition, don't ever believe or be deceived that the way you are now is the best you can ever be! There is more in you than you can ever see. The devil knows this. That is why he doesn't stop attacking people because he knows you can and would rise again.

With faith in God and a right attitude, you can stop the enemy in his tracks. You can tell him to his face that you won't give in or give up.

A right attitude tells you that being broke financially does not mean you are finally broken. It helps to tell the enemy that having less does not mean you are less.

A right attitude helps you to patiently wait for God's timing, and it builds your courage. It helps you to believe in your tomorrow and it fires your enthusiasm to want to excel.

A right attitude helps you embrace joy in the face of challenges, and it imbues you with a confidence to press on in spite of tough times.

Your faith in Christ and a right attitude will embolden you to trust God and surrender all to Him. It would kill pride, which is a secret ally of the devil working against God's children.

Remember that pride will turn God against you. If the devil cannot get you to steal, fornicate or commit other sins, he would try you with pride. And once you fall for his bait, you can no longer resist or silence his voice against your life.

> *"But He gives more grace. Therefore He says: "God resists the proud, But gives grace to the humble." [7] Therefore submit to God. Resist the devil and he will flee from you"*
> *(James 4: 6-7, NKJV)*

If you must overcome the enemy, you must first walk with God and subject yourself to Him.

"Humble yourselves in the sight of the Lord, and he shall lift you up" (James 4: 10)

DECLARATIONS / PRAYERS

1. Oh Lord, whatever will make me doubt your purpose; take them away, in Jesus' name.

2. At the moment when I don't understand your purpose for me, Lord give me the grace to trust your wisdom.

3. Heavenly Father, I am clay in your hands, remould my life to your glory, in Jesus' name.

4. Oh Lion of The Tribe of Judah, harass and destroy every lion harassing my life!

5. Heavenly Father, give me the grace to live a life that is pleasing and acceptable to you.

6. Every hidden character and attitude problem hindering my life, Oh Lord take them away!

7. The source of faithlessness and disobedience in my life, Father turn them around, in Jesus' name.

8. Whatsoever is hiding in my life and cooperating with the enemy to hinder my destiny, Oh Lord, expose and disgrace them, in Jesus' name!

Last Word:

The True Power Over The Enemy!

Your ultimate power to overcome the enemy and the attendant challenge of life is determined by whom you belong to.

The victory to overcome the enemy is tied to the shield covering you and the faith you profess.

The Bible says, *"The name of the LORD is a strong tower: the righteous runneth into it, and is safe" (Pro 18: 10).*

The name of Jesus protects and it lifts you out of the reach of the enemy. You only need to believe and receive Him and He would empower you.

"But as many as received him, to them gave he power to become the sons of God, even to them that believe on his name" (John 1: 12)

"For whatsoever is born of God overcometh the world: and this is the victory that overcometh the world, even our faith. ⁵ Who is he that overcometh the world, but he that believeth that Jesus is the Son of God?" (1 John 5: 4-5)

May the Lord permanently silence all the enemies of your life in Jesus' name. Amen!

Salvation: The Key To Victory

"Come unto me all ye that labour and are heavy laden and I will give you rest" (Matt11:28).

The key to ultimately become victorious in life and become what God wants you to be is to accept the Lord Jesus Christ as your Lord and personal Saviour.

If you want to accept Him right now and qualify to receive the grace and glory God has promised, then read aloud and confess the following prayer, and accept it as true:

Dear Heavenly Father, in response to your word, I come to you in the name of Jesus -for a new beginning.

Your Word says, "...him that cometh to me I will in no wise cast out" (John 6:37), so I have the confidence that You won't cast me out, but You would accept me.

I pray and ask Jesus to come into my heart and be Lord over my life. And I give you all the glory.

I believe and confess that Jesus Christ is the Son of God and the Lord. I believe that He was raised from the dead for my justification. According to Your word "...with the heart man believeth unto righteousness..." and I do believe with my heart, I am now a child of God. I am saved. Praise the Lord!

Ben E. Efe, the Senior Pastor of LivingWater Int'l Ministries (Grace Centre) and president of Stay Alive Int'l. He is an avid teacher of the Word with passion for making believers live the abundant life promised by the Lord and becoming all that God wants them to be.

His practical and insightful teaching helps to keep souls miles ahead of the devil whilst enjoying the abundant grace made available by the Lord Jesus Christ. This forms the fulcrum of Stay Alive - John 10:10.

Ben is available for ministration and engagement in churches, conferences and other meetings aimed at blessing souls.

For enquiries, kindly contact:

LivingWater Int'l Ministries (Grace Centre):
P. O. Box 22626, Ikeja, Lagos, Nigeria
e-mail: livingwater_intl@yahoo.com;
stayalive_intl@yahoo.com
http://www.stayalivetips.blogspot.com
+234-803 512 5496, 802 930 9859
+234-805 866 6643

Some Other Books By Ben E. Efe

"The Successful Believer": affirms the believer's right and authority. It exposes the weaknesses and game plan of the devil. It offers spiritual and biblical keys for overcoming the enemy and living a fruitful Christian life. If you have ever been frustrated, defeated, discouraged, afflicted and fearful, but now ready for a change, then this book is for you!

Wings Of A Dove (Overcoming Fear & Discouragement): exposes and demystifies fear and its problems, and it offers keys to make your fears fear you! If you have ever been afraid, under-fire, hopeless, discouraged, frustrated, betrayed, but ready to live victoriously, here is your chance. Come on board and win! This book will take you to a new level. It would change your life!

"Hands On The Plough..." This book offers tips to handle the challenges of part time ministry. It is born out of a practical experience to help ministers grapple with the pressures of office work, societal, family and other needs, and at the same time serve effectively in the Master's Vineyard. It is recommended for ministers, pastors, Bible College students and all believers.

Some Other Books By Ben E. Efe

"10 Vital Vitamins To Turn Your Life Around!"
The fall of a man is not the end of his life! This book offers 10 keys to help you overcome setbacks, discouragement, failure and the challenges of life. It will help you to turn your life around, to become the fulfilled person God created you to be!

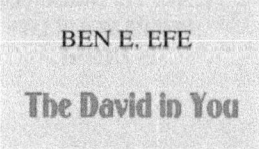

**"The David in You!
...Making Your Gifts & Potentials Work For You".**
There is a light inside of you - a gift, a potential that would make you shine, if you switch it on. This little book would help you make that greatness in you work for you.

**"ABC...
Biblical Steps To Success & Fulfillment!"**
Success does not come by accident! It involves taking positive steps with faith hinged on God.

This book will give you the A - Z of what you need to become successful in life and become the person whom God ordained you to be.

Some Other Books By Ben E. Efe

"12 Ways To Discover Where Your Life is Going"

God created you with a purpose. But many people do not discover their essence and live dissatisfied and unfulfilled lives. This book will help you discover your true self and reveal where your life is heading now.

"Redeemed For Glory!"

This book offers concise biblical analyses to proffer solutions to seemingly difficult questions affecting our faith. It will give hope to the hopeless and strength to the weak.

It is a must-read for all who desire to know their stand in Christ!

Some Other Books By Ben E. Efe

"12 Men & Their Wives"

It is good to dream of a sweet and happy marriage. But a dream is not enough. Successful marriage comes by choice - hard work, sacrifice, patience and love. This book will give you biblical insights and tips to help you build a successful and fulfilling marriage and expose pitfall and dangers you must avoid. It is a must-read for couples and all intending to get married!

"KIIL THAT god"

(Simple Ways To Overcome Bad Habits & Addictions)

This book will help you to overcome wrong habits and indulgences. It would help you make that change to kill the gods behind the habits and addictions troubling your life!

www.ingramcontent.com/pod-product-compliance
Lightning Source LLC
Chambersburg PA
CBHW071744040426
42446CB00012B/2472